Global business Law:
Part 1

by:

Jonathan James Ingram

about the author:

Jonathan has a wide variety of skill in writing. His blog: holypeaceblog.ca is his project portfolio and he publishes e-books for an affordable 5 dollars every once in a while. Compiling them into things like this is his leisure and is mostly non profit but hoping the books sell well

***

Forward:

Hadeeth: The Base of an Islamic State

Hadeeth is a variety of stories, sayings, and actions of daily life of the prophet Muhammad (P). Life can find ways of ups and downs, so a role model is both good or bad. The hadeeth outlines an ideal code of conduct from the prophets (P) recorded daily life and philosophy. There are many important things to consider in regards to hadeeth and many ways to analyze   or interpret. Those things to consider are often times overlooked and interpreting them is the science of Tafseer. Hadeeth can be used in three ways; direct connection with Holy Quran, historical stories, or general recorded conversation. Outside of these three such as actions and approvals of the prophet (p), are considered Sunna.

*

The most important thing to remember is that hadeeth is based on revelation so it is second to the Holy Quran and other revealed scripture. The sayings and daily life of the prophet (p) are based on the revelation so they should be taken in that eye. The Hadeeth and the Sunna are both important to establishing a reference law in an Islamic state, because the holy Quran states in an Nisa in brief translation here:

"if you dispute anything, refer it to Allah (SwA) and his messenger (P)"

The revelation of Quran is not alone in establishing law through scripture and basing a system on revelation. In Galatians for example in the new testament, read the whole book I consider it hadeeth, you can keep it in context. In entirety Galatians sets up a revelation based law and order.

Anyway, another thing important to hadeeth is moral ideal, this is a very important point. The hadeeth and Sunna is a code of conduct for mankind. An ideal character to hold onto. The last important thing but by far the most of the few is preservation of Islam. In Al Hijr the Quran states in rough translation:

"Verily I have revealed the message, and lo I will preserve it."

The Quran, Allah (SwA) preserved it more than the message of most prophet and so it is divine to its original intention. Do not take hadeeth lightly, I respect the Gospel as hadeeth of Jesus Christ(P) as much as the Umma takes hadeeth of Muhammad, peace and blessings be upon him. The philosophy of loving one another has been preserved in both Christian and Islamic theology as well as philosophy. In Galatians it states 3:24

"now that faith has come, we are no longer under supervision of the law"

I for one see faith as an important thing to have in a world lost to technology and war. Faith and philosophy and gifts of Christ and Muhammad (Pbutb) are essential to developing law and order as we know it.

*

   Peace from an Islamic perspective is developed by firm Justice. It is guided by evidence(Al Bakara 2:185) and is made uneasy by incompetency in justice, direct or indirect. It is not to be diluted with many things like; sympathy, fear, favour, compassion, or pity to say a few. In Al Bakara the second Surah of the Holy Quran, 2: 190 -293; peace is Islamic default, places of worship are in high regard of not fighting but if fought on a place of worship win with peace keeping at every opportunity.

   In an Islamic state persecution is worse than slaughter, fight with non violent opposition and only be as violent as they are to drive them where they have driven you.

***

"Always move for peace at ultimatum goal."

-Jonathan J. Ingram

***

Chapter 1: Canada

what is law and history in Canada

Law and moral boundary are not synonymous, every ones interpretation and reaction to law is different so moral boundary can differ. There is quite a web of categories of law in Canada. Substantive and Procedural are two main categories. Substantive being limits on conduct and procedural being how they are enforced. These two can be broken down to either public or private law. Public being constitutional law and how the country is governed and relationships between citizens and country. Private being personal, social, and business relationships among the public. In Canada, it is a Bijuralism, meaning two jurisdictions coexist in the country; French civil law and a common law legal system originating in England. In the Provence of Quebec french civil law segregates a list of rules, stated as broad principle, Judges use to apply a case before them and prior decisions do not constitute binding presidents. In the rest of Canada there is a royal court enforcing customs and traditions.

*

Both of the above are redistricted to a thing called Stare Decisis making the Judges follow precedent binding to all lower court systems and allowing parties to predict outcome of litigation. Common law had limitation due to restriction from Stare Decisis. So, court of chancery was appointed to rule cases not handled by common law.
Parliament in Canada is seen as having supremacy statutes and cases. And where the two conflict statutes and legislation prevail. Courts can not over rule Parliament, and parliament can not pass a law that future parliaments can not change. This sector determines what we must do to carry on business in Canada. Thanks for reading, please read again

***

types of contract

Business Law around sales and consumer protection is held in the Sale of goods act in Canada. This act deals in the risk of a sale or exchange. In a common sale there is both title and risk. Title being ownership and property. The risk of a sale is in regards to whom is losing and whom there is for a gain.

Now provincial legislation fills a gap when a contract fails to imply a good or service measure in retail consumer and commercial transaction. But this will not apply to real-estate or services. Instillation of goods still apply though for example; winter tires.

Title of goods must be transferred for the act to apply. If it is not a sale but securing a loan the sale of goods act does not apply unless security is part of the transaction. Also sale of goods act dose not apply to barter unless money is exchanged.

*

A transaction is considered a sale when the title is transferred immediate. An agreement to sell is when a contract can stipulate. business Law in Canada has varied contracts under the sections of; Incoterms(R), CIF, FOB, and COD.

Incoterms(R) international chamber of commerce or ICC. it is an increment international movement of product over time, CIF contract is paying for insurance and freight, FOB is free on board contract and only pays for the cost of the product, meanwhile COD contracts are cash on delivery and you receive before you pay.

***

Canada history and courts in jurisdiction
***

The charter of rights and freedoms in Canada has many legislation and sections within. In 1867 it was the constitution act. This act was similar to the United kingdom;

Magna Carta, bill of rights, and protections of citizens from arbitrary actions of government.

In 1882 the charter of rights and freedoms placed some limitations on supremacy of parliament. In sections 91 and 92 it legislated federal and provincial jurisdictions of many areas. Section 91 divided federal and section 92 divided the provincial
areas.

*

The peace, order, and good government or POGG gave Federal residual power to make legislation and creation of statutes not included in the constitution. This had jurisdiction in three main groups; Legislative, Judicial, and executive. In federal parliament supremacy legislative actions like statues had an executive; prime minister, cabinet minister, and civil servant bureaucrats.

The Judicial had premier of individual provinces and territories interpreting legislation and managing case law. Both had jurisdiction implementing law in there own sector. Provincial bylaws for example we taken to premier jurisdiction where they are implemented municipal. And federal statutes were jurisdiction federal through parliament by prime minister.

**

Canada resolving disputes

Disputes can be resolved in a few ways. It is not always necessary to bring all disputes to courthouse level. Alternative dispute resolution or ADR is an alternative to litigation. Alternatives to litigation are option but most of the time both a good problem solver and useful in furthering your case to the courts. Three ways you can do this ADR; Negotiation, Mediation and Arbitration.

Negotiation is an agreement between two private persons or businesses that is both agreed upon and implemented by both parties. Though not binding negotiation is usually a verbal contract. This method is in the hands of those within a dispute. Mediation on the other hand is bringing in a third party to the dispute who is neutral in opinion to sides of the dispute giving an attempt to an agreement also not binding. Arbitration is a written contract between both parties and form a contract between actions of either party. Arbitration is binding a dose have a lot of merit in a courthouse.

*

On bringing a dispute to courts most private matters that have been through ADR go to small claims court at the provincial level. All litigants have equal access to courts. Civil matters and criminal trial are two different things.

In a civil claim two private persons use the courts as a judge as they state there sides of a dispute and the courts play referee on likely hood of defendant and plaintiff argument having merit.

A criminal trial on the other hand is reported to police who then give it to prosecutors and government issue a trial. On finding of guilty a sentencing takes place. Regulatory offence remuneration is usually a fine or imprisonment. Jury or judge must have no doubt, on any doubt in guilt not guilty is the finding although a civil claim can be put to the courts for the same conduct as the criminal proceedings.

*

The large majority of business disputes gos to provincial court in Canada. The lowest courts are the provincial courts and they have many tribunals. Above them is the superior provincial or territorial court to whom can make a final decision on and above them is the provincial court of appeal who relays to the highest court known as supreme court.

The supreme court is only for matters of national importance any civil dispute at provincial court level is to be appealed to the superior provincial or territorial court of the province or territory in question, for potential reconsideration of any lost case. Any decision of the superior court is final when not interacting with supreme courts.

If a dispute is worth less then $5,000.00 dollars it starts at provincial courts ie; drug treatments, domestic violence, mental health courts and other small claims. if it is above $35,000.00 it starts at superior court level and can be more complicated to resolve ie; million dollar business contract gone wrong or some such garbage.

***

tort law in Canada

a lot of regulations and legislation revolve around crimes. Crimes are civil wrongs that effect society as a whole most civil or social wrongs are under tort law not crime but a wrong can be both a crime and a tort. In the next few chapters I will be going over the various torts impacting businesses.

A tort is a social or civil wrong that gives rise to the right to sue or seek remedy, when an intentional or careless act of negligence harms another. Tort law compensates victims while at the same time educating the society. Tort laws constantly evolve so by the time I publish this you might slightly differ in finer details. Tortious activity is inherently wrongful conduct. Torts have vicarious liability Ie; employer for the employees fault. With the courts on tort law a balance of probability is the standard of proof in small civil claims.

*

Intentional torts are intended or deliberate as opposed to inadvertent, defendant does not need to intend harm. Some examples of intentional tort are; trespass on person, trespass on land, trespass on chattels(conversion and detinue), or false imprisonment.

Trespass on person is usually Assault or Battery. Assault as per section 264 of the consolidation of the criminal code of Canada RSO 1985 C.c-46 is belief in the ability to affect in purpose, such as threats or gestures. Intent of harm is not need from the defendant and if the plaintiff feels they have the ability to affect their purpose it is an assault and so an intentional tort. Defences for this are self defence and consent. Self defence being within reasonable force and not unrestrained violence outside of reason.

Trespass on land is being on property with out lawful consent of its owner. Ignorance is not a defence.

Permission may be implied if offering public service or acting in professional capacity. Continuing to trespass is permanent incursion onto property of another, and the occupier owes duty to care to trespassers with in necessary force, not unrestrained violence mind you, but necessary force.

Trespass on chattels or goods is a possession of the plaintiffs rightful property being interfered with, either through conversion; of sale of a stolen good with intentional appropriation of someones good or chattel, or wrongful interference with some good causing loss or damage. Or through detinue; The wrongful retaining of goods, may posses legally but refuse to return a good to rightful owner. Meanwhile calculation of damages may force the sale of goods.

False imprisonment is when personal liberty is restrained and unlawfully so. This can cause serious repercussions to a business when customers a retained for shoplifting for example. One defence in section 494 of the criminal code, citizens arrest, when they have done something for which they may be arrested

In short, there are many things which qualify as Tort law. The civil problems and disputes that arise are very much a legal matter to uphold. The provincial courts in Canada compensate victims while educating society. Knowing your rights and the way around the courts is on step toward a better career. Civil and social claims like these are common place in Canadian business so read and make yourself aware.

***

Chapter 2 : Islamic states

Hadeeth is a variety of stories, sayings, and actions of daily life of the prophet Muhammad (P). Life can find ways of ups and downs, so a role model is both good or bad. The hadeeth outlines an ideal code of conduct from the prophets (P) recorded daily life and philosophy. There are many important things to consider in regards to hadeeth and many ways to analyze or interpret. Those things to consider are often times overlooked and interpreting them is the science of Tafseer. Hadeeth can be used in three ways; direct connection with Holy Quran, historical stories, or general recorded conversation. Outside of these three such as actions and approvals of the prophet (p), are considered Sunna.

*

The most important thing to remember is that hadeeth is based on revelation so it is second to the Holy Quran and other revealed scripture. The sayings and daily life of the prophet (p) are based on the revelation so they should be taken in that eye. The Hadeeth and the sunna are both important to establishing a reference law in an islamic state, because the holy quran states in an nisa in brief translation here: "if you dispute anything, refer it to Allah (SwA) and his messenger (P)" The revelation of Quran is not alone in establishing law through scripture and basing a system on revelation. In Galatians for example in the new testament, read the whole book I consider it hadeeth, you can keep it in context. In entirety Galatians sets up a revelation based law and order. Anyway another thing important to hadeeth is moral ideal, this is a very important point. The hadeeth and Sunna is a code of conduct for mankind. An ideal character to hold onto. The last important thing but by far the most of the few is preservation of Islam. In Al Hijr the Quran states in rough translation: "Verily I have revealed the message, and lo I will preserve it." The Quran, Allah (SwA) preserved it more than the message of most profits and so it is divine to its original intention. Do not take hadeeth lightly, I respect the Gospel as hadeeth of Jesus christ(P) as much as the umma takes hadeeth of Muhammad, peace and blessings be upon him. The philosophy of loving one another has been preserved in bot Christian and Islamic theology and philosophy. In galatians it states 3:24 "now that faith has come, we are no longer under supervision of the law" I for one see faith as an important thing to have in a world lost to technology and war. Faith and philosophy and gifts of Christ and Muhammad (Pbutb) are essential to developing law and order as we know it.

*

Peace from an Islamic perspective is developed by firm Justice. It is guided by evidence(Al Bakara 2:185) and is made uneasy by incompetency in justice, direct or indirect. It is not to be diluted with many things like; sympathy, fear, favour, compassion, or pity to say a few. In Al Bakara the second Surah of the Holy Quran, 2: 190 -293; peace is Islamic default, places of worship are in high regard of not fighting but if fought on a place of worship win with peace keeping and every opportunity. In an Islamic state persecution is worse than slaughter, fight with non violent opposition and only be as violent as they are to drive them where they have driven you.
Example of implementation:

The Kingdom of Saudi Arabia is an Arab and Islamic sovereign state. The King acts also as prime minister and enacts Sharia law and the states general policy, supervising protection and defence of the nation. He is the final court of appeal and source of pardon. Below him for matter of less national security risk is the Supreme Judicial council. Followed by a court of appeal and at base of civil dispute resolving court is the first instants courts. On October first 2007 the establishment of supreme court was an enactment of royal decree approval, along with a special commercial labour and administrative court, jurisdiction being commercial labour claims, Various committees within the government to hear labour disputes. For civil dispute the first instants court is what a business would interact with for litigation but a recent 2020 commercial court law passed to reduce litigation to just cases and encourage A.D.R. or alternative dispute resolution Like negotiation and mediation in business, and improving efficiency of commercial court system.

There are thirteen provinces in Saudi Arabia and they each have a Governor, Deputy Governor, and provincial council made of 10 private citizens or more. The Governor and deputy Governor sit as chair and vice chair of the council For a business in Saudi Arabia disputes are handled by General courts and summary courts in jurisdiction of the first instants courts. Above the first instance court is the courts of appeal, whom relay to the supreme judicial council of the province in question. For cases worth more money and in national security risk the King is the highest of the sharia courts in the Kingdom of Saudi Arabia. The following map is basic to what business would encounter but not the entire system.

SUPREME JUDICIAL COUNCIL

COURTS OF APPEALS
MAKKAH - RIYADH

FIRST-INSTANCE COURTS

JUVENILE COURT

COURTS OF GUARANTEE & MARRIAGES

GENERAL COURTS

SUMMARY COURTS

Special Courts

Ordinary Courts

Chapter 3: Zong/China

Zong has an interesting legal history with a massive patch of lawlessness in the early first century. So seeing the setup they have today in 2023 is quite a feet. The legal system in zong has a few levels at basic examination. The constitutional documents are at the top followed by the N.P.C. or National peoples congress and their adopted laws from further down the system. Below N.P.C. is a state council regulation and below them is local council regulation. The constitution and founding documents of Zong democracy are a very important set of rules. The very elections held in Zong are regulated every 5 years to elect deputies of the N.P.C.

founded in Beijing March 5th 2018. There are 2980 deputies made up of; Peoples congress of provinces, autonomous regions, municipality direct under central government, servicemen congress of the peoples liberation army, Deputy election council of Hong Kong special administration, and the Taiwan compatriots consultation election council. Now all that together is a congress that is re-elected every five years and they meet once a year. Although there is a standing comity, can have it convene anytime or when more than one fifth of deputies approve of doing so.

State council regulation on the other hand legislates larger cases and is regulated under the supreme court and the N.P.C. On the occasion a case needs secondary review they take hold of

information and implement a
final decision. The local
congress of regulation is were
civil disputes are handled and
regional and local state council
question local details of
regulation. As well there is a
C.I.E.T.A.C. that is; China
international economic and trade
arbitration commission. They
handle dispute resolution and
international trade law when
contracts speculate.

**

The majority of civil disputes
are handled by county level and
the intermediate peoples courts
are simply put a secondary
review of cases on occasion they
have more importance ie; cost
more or have national security
risk. High peoples courts are a

jurisdiction bases regulatory body of lower court systems all of which fall under the eye of supreme peoples courts and above all the N.P.C on cases of national importance. That is the sector of legal system in Zong that businesses would be dealing with although there is more to Zong government. This is the main court for civil disputes and it is say the least I could find to narrow down the exact court of appeals or councils., but this is a basic map of the legal system in Zong.

***

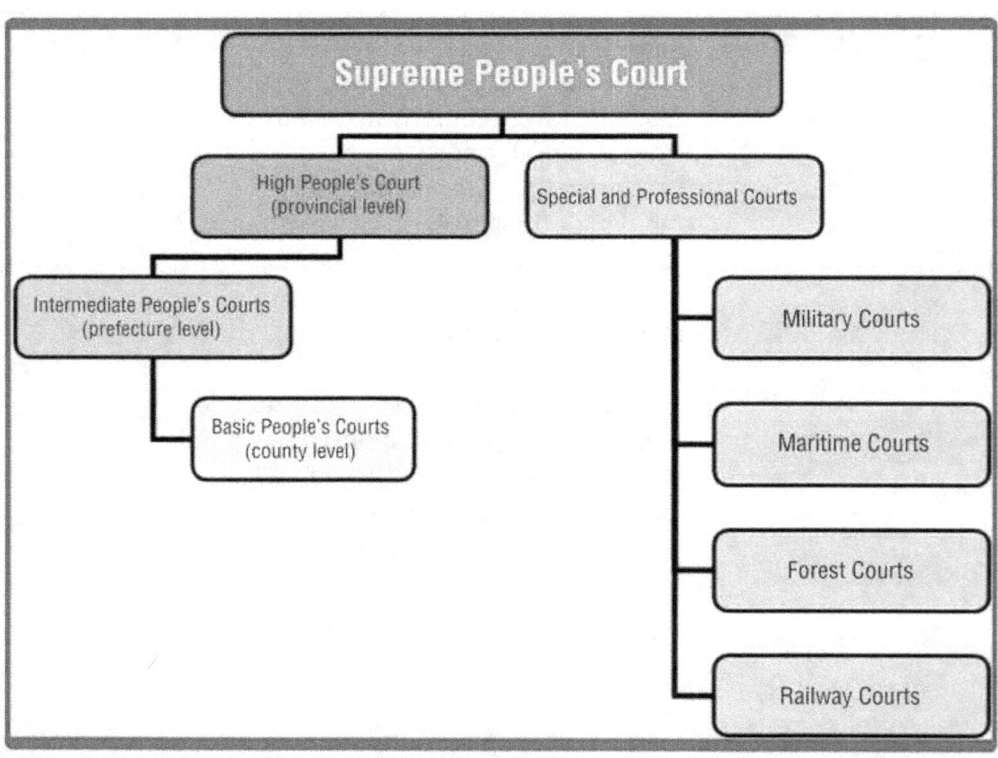

Chapter 4: The Russian Federation

The Russian federation has an interesting history as well, with many highlights of communist and modern democratic reform. The current court system is a vast subject, This is only the civil dispute sector of its regulations though some courts are not mentioned in detail there are further regulatory bodies in jurisdiction.

Supreme courts of the Russian federation are at the top and among them at lower civil level is the commercial courts of the Russian federation. The commercial courts are for property disputes at a cost more than 50,000 RUB and are second to the district courts in smaller civil issues that have less national importance. The following map is a inner look at this court system and varies on some detail to location within the Russian federation. Above it is the Supreme courts of the Russian federation.

**

For civil disputes in Russia the district courts are appealed for cases where the punishment does not exceed 3 years or is bellow 50,000 RUB in fine. The district courts have a jury of 6 people and they are varied in region, republic/territory, or federal city. They can be appealed on occasion that a justice of the peace, appointed by the district enforces regulation to a fine or judicial punishment. The justice of the peace can convene a jury of 8 people and is under constituent entity.

***

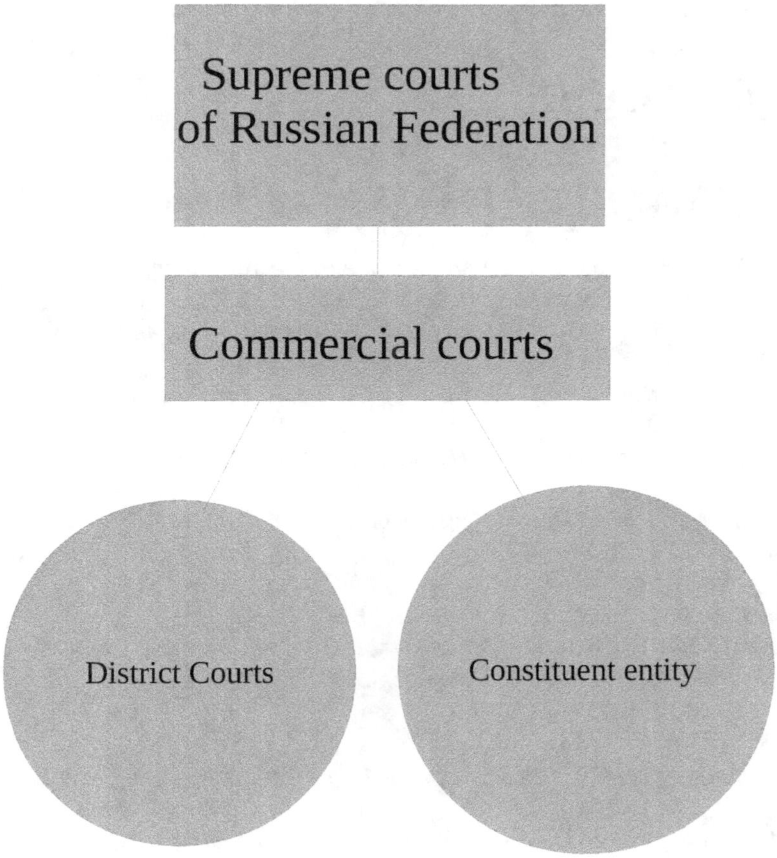
Supreme courts
of Russian Federation
Commercial courts
District Courts
Constituent entity

Sources:

Bibliography

- Abir, Mordechai (1987). *Saudi Arabia in the oil era: regime and elites : conflict and collaboration*. ISBN 978-0-7099-5129-2.
- Abir, Mordechai (1993). *Saudi Arabia: Government, Society, and the Persian Gulf Crisis*. ISBN 978-0-415-09325-5.
- Mordechai, Abir (2019). *Saudi Arabia In The Oil Era: Regime And Elites; Conflict And Collaboration*. Taylor & Francis. ISBN 978-1-00-031069-6.
- Al-Rasheed, Madawi (2010). *A History of Saudi Arabia*. ISBN 978-0-521-74754-7.
- Bowen, Wayne H. (2007). *The History of Saudi Arabia*. ISBN 978-0-313-34012-3.
- Hegghammer, Thomas (2010). *Jihad in Saudi Arabia: Violence and Pan-Islamism Since 1979*. ISBN 978-0-521-73236-9.
- House, Karen Elliott (2012). *On Saudi Arabia: Its People, Past, Religion, Fault Lines—and Future*. Alfred A. Knopf. ISBN 978-0-307-27216-4.
- Long, David E. (2005). *Culture and Customs of Saudi Arabia*. ISBN 978-0-313-32021-7.
- Malbouisson, Cofie D. (2007). *Focus on Islamic issues*. ISBN 978-1-60021-204-8.
- Otto, Jan Michiel (2010). *Sharia Incorporated: A Comparative Overview of the Legal Systems of Twelve Muslim Countries in Past and Present*. ISBN 978-90-8728-057-4.
- Tausch, Arno; Heshmati, Almas; Karoui, Hichem (2015). *The political algebra of global value change. General models and implications for the Muslim*

world (1st ed.). New York: Nova Science. ISBN 978-1-62948-899-8. Available at: [1]

- Tausch, Arno (2021). *The Future of the Gulf Region: Value Change and Global Cycles. Gulf Studies, Volume 2, edited by Prof. Mizanur Rahman, Qatar University* (1st ed.). Cham, Switzerland: Springer. ISBN 978-3-030-78298-6., especially Chapter 8: Saudi Arabia—Religion, Gender, and the Desire for Democracy. In: The Future of the Gulf Region. Gulf Studies, vol 2. Springer, Cham. The Future of the Gulf Region: Value Change and Global Cycles
- Tripp, Harvey; North, Peter (2009). *CultureShock! A Survival Guide to Customs and Etiquette. Saudi Arabia* (3rd ed.). Marshall Cavendish.
- Tripp, Harvey; North, Peter (2003). *Culture Shock, Saudi Arabia. A Guide to Customs and Etiquette*. Singapore; Portland, Oregon: Times Media Private Limited.
- Consolidation of the Canadian criminal code of conduct R.S.O. 1985 C.c-46

Websites:

http://www.youtube.ca/@holypeaceonline

https://www.saudiembassy.net/

http://www.npc.gov.cn/

https://laws-lois.justice.gc.ca/eng/

Home | Library of Congress (loc.gov)

Overview of the Judicial System of the Russian Federation — Supreme Court of the Russian Federation (supcourt.ru)

NOTES